Original title:

Pale Cords Beneath the Elf Turf

Author: Kene Elistrand

ISBN HARDBACK: 978-1-80563-180-4

ISBN PAPERBACK: 978-1-80564-701-0

The Echoing Roots of Time

In the whispers of the ancient trees,
Memories drift on the cool, soft breeze.
Shadows dance where the sunlight falls,
Time itself speaks in the echoing calls.

Through the depths of night's silent roam,
Each star a tale, each journey a home.
Threads of history in the moon's gentle light,
Binding the past to the dreams of the night.

Beneath the soil, the secrets lie,
Roots intertwine with a soft, knowing sigh.
As seasons shift, the stories unfold,
In the circle of life, fate's tapestry told.

A whisper of magic in every heartbeat,
Echoes of laughter, the past bittersweet.
Carried on winds that refuse to grow old,
Each moment a treasure, a memory to hold.

Awake in the dusk, when dusk meets the dawn,
Lost in the spell of this endless yawn.
For time is an echo, a dance in the mist,
And roots of the past persist to exist.

Echoes of the Forest's Hearth

In the heart of the woods, where the shadows play,
Whispers of magic lead the lost astray.
The flicker of firelight, warm on the skin,
Invites the heart, where the tales begin.

Beneath a canopy, emerald and bright,
Creatures of wonder take wing in the night.
Rustling leaves sing the old bard's song,
As echoes of laughter grow joyful and strong.

Around the hearth, stories weave and wend,
Of heroes and hearts and the wounds they mend.
In shadows long cast, where memories bloom,
The magic of kinship dispels the gloom.

With every ember that glows in the dark,
A spark of adventure ignites with a mark.
Through thickets and brambles, we journey afar,
Guided by starlight, our wishes a star.

So gather, dear friends, by the fire's embrace,
Where echoes of joy in this sacred space.
In the forest's warm hearth, all fears take flight,
And the bonds that we forge shine eternally bright.

Dance of Dust and Dew

In morning's light, the whispers play,
On golden beams, the sparkles sway.
With every step, the shadows twirl,
As nature wakes, in magic's swirl.

The breezes hum, in rhythmic tune,
While droplets dance, 'neath silver moon.
A symphony of soft delight,
Unfolding dreams in purest sight.

Around the glade, the fairies flutter,
Through blades of grass, their laughter splutter.
With every flick, the spark lights glow,
In gentle waltz, they ebb and flow.

The petals blush with dawn's embrace,
As morning dew takes on its place.
In stillness found, the world awakes,
To weave the magic that nature makes.

Marvels in the Mossy Tibers

Beneath the trees, where shadows rest,
In mossy beds, the secrets nest.
With whispers soft, the Tibers sing,
Of hidden wonders, life can bring.

A tapestry of emerald hues,
With stories old and ancient clues.
Each fern a tale, each stone a song,
In woven realms where dreams belong.

The sunlight sparkles, a jeweled gown,
As whispers weave through leafy crown.
A gentle touch, a fleeting breeze,
Unlocking tales among the trees.

Through twilight's veil, the secrets glide,
In mossy nooks, where shadows hide.
They beckon forth to hearts anew,
To dance among the verdant view.

In every rustle, a life takes flight,
A symphony beneath the night.
In mossy tibers, marveled beams,
Awake the world with silent dreams.

Fables of the Twilit Grove

In twilight's hold, the stories weave,
Through branches thin, the dreams believe.
A fable born of dusk and dawn,
In whispered tones, the night has drawn.

The owls recount the tales of old,
Of heroes brave and spirits bold.
With every sigh of mossy ground,
The echoes rise, a magic found.

Glowing fae with laughter light,
Illuminate the stars of night.
In unity, the shadows blend,
A tapestry with no clear end.

The moonlight spills on ancient stone,
In this embrace, we're never alone.
With every breeze, a voice remains,
In fables told when twilight reigns.

A journey shared, the heart's delight,
In twilit grove, where dreams take flight.
The fables call, as night descends,
In magic's arms, the soul transcends.

Fractured Light in Enchanted Places

Through tangled vines, the sunlight breaks,
In laughter soft, the heart awakes.
With every glint, a spark ignites,
In woven realms of secret sights.

Fractured light on leaves will dance,
In gentle sway, a wisp of chance.
Like fleeting whispers on the air,
It carries dreams beyond compare.

In enchanted nooks, the shadows play,
While twilight hues dissolve the day.
A ballet of the night unfurls,
As magic twirls in secret swirls.

With every step, the world in bloom,
Exudes a scent of sweet perfume.
A tapestry of glimmering rays,
In fractured light, we lose our gaze.

So linger here, where wonders flare,
In enchanted places, hearts laid bare.
With fractured light, our spirits soar,
In realms where magic is evermore.

Luminescent Echoes in the Quiet

In the hush of twilight's breath,
Stars awaken, casting light.
Soft whispers dance on dusky winds,
Carrying dreams into the night.

Moonlit paths weave through the gloom,
Secrets linger, soft and bright.
Echoes shimmer in the dark,
Painting visions out of sight.

Among the shadows, stories flow,
Each flicker tells a tale anew.
With every pulse, the world awakes,
Awash in silver, calm and true.

Through the quiet, echoes sing,
Of distant realms and ancient lore.
Where light and shadow intertwine,
Revealing magic evermore.

So gather round, ye dreamers bold,
In twilight's clutch, let spirits soar.
For in the silence, hearts ignite,
In luminescent echoes' core.

Cradled Secrets of the Forest's Heart

Deep within the emerald maze,
Whispers flutter on the breeze.
Each leaf holds tales of olden days,
Gardens nurtured by ancient trees.

In twilight's cloak, where shadows play,
Mysteries weave through roots and stones.
The forest breathes a sacred hymn,
Cradling secrets in mossy thrones.

Beneath the boughs, the faeries dance,
Starlight glimmers on dew-kissed ferns.
Echoes of laughter and chance,
In every branch, the magic churns.

The wild things stir, the hidden paths,
In moonlit glades, their secrets throng.
With every rustle, life begins,
And nature hums its timeless song.

So wander forth, ye seekers brave,
Embrace the forest's gentle sigh.
For in its heart, the stories wait,
A cradle where the wild things lie.

The Intertwined Weft of Faerie Dreams

In twilight's weave, soft visions rise,
Threads of gossamer, spun from light.
Faerie dreams in silver skies,
Entwine the stars with whispered flight.

Amidst the glow of twilight's gleam,
A tapestry of hopes unfolds.
Every moment, a glistening dream,
Weaving magic from stories told.

In hidden nooks where shadows lie,
The fae play tricks, mischievous and free.
With twinkling laughter, they softly sigh,
Binding hearts in woven glee.

Each flicker of light, a secret shared,
In every flutter, love's embrace.
With every dream, a soul laid bare,
In the maze of ethereal grace.

So let your heart be open wide,
To the weft where dreams arise.
For in the faerie's playful tide,
Life's sweetest magic ever lies.

Whispers of the Rooted Realm

In the depths where shadows dwell,
The rooted realm breathes tales away.
Murmurs echo like a spell,
Hidden truths in soft decay.

Among the brambles, stories speak,
Of time immemorial, crushed and frail.
Through fragile breaths, the ancients seek,
To weave their dreams within the pale.

With every rustle in the leaves,
The spirits rise, both fierce and shy.
They share their wisdom, if one believes,
In whispers where the memories lie.

So pause and listen to the ground,
Where roots entwine and hearts revive.
In every sigh, a bond is found,
In whispers, the rooted realm survives.

Embrace the stories nature keeps,
For in her arms, we grow anew.
The rooted realm in silence leaps,
A dance of life, both old and true.

An Ode to the Elusive Spirits

In shadows deep where whispers play,
The spirits dance in twilight's sway.
They flit like dreams from mind's embrace,
A fleeting glimpse, a phantom grace.

With laughter soft as midnight's breath,
They weave their tales of life and death.
In silver light, they twirl and spin,
The echoes of the world within.

They beckon hearts to chase the night,
Their secrets wrapped in silken light.
Each flicker fuels the daring quest,
To know the realms where spirits rest.

In woods where sunlight seldom shows,
The ancient knowledge, softly flows.
Through hidden glades the whispers roam,
In every sigh, a tale of home.

Yet who can grasp these fleeting forms,
When daylight breaks, and quiet norms.
In dreams we find them, soft and rare,
An ode to them, a whispered prayer.

Moonlit Paths of the Enchanted

Beneath the glow of silver beams,
The forest sings of ancient dreams.
Where moonlight weaves through leaves that sway,
The night unfurls in soft ballet.

Along the paths where shadows blend,
The echoes of the night transcend.
With every step, the magic grows,
In moonlit dances, joy bestows.

The owls call out with dulcet tones,
As secrets bared like whispered moans.
In harmony, the night aligns,
An orchestra of stars that shines.

The brook's soft laugh in gentle stride,
Guides wayward souls through bramble wide.
With every turn, a heart may find,
The wonders lost to waking mind.

So roam the paths where magic thrives,
And welcome all the spirit lives.
In moonlit glow, a world reborn,
A tapestry of night adorned.

Sprite Echoes in the Stillness

In the hush of dawn, where breezes sigh,
The sprites emerge, with laughter nigh.
A shimmer here, a giggle there,
They weave through dreams like fragrant air.

With wings of gossamer, they glide,
In whispered games, they love to hide.
Between the ferns, in sunlight's gleam,
A flicker caught, as if a dream.

They speak in tunes of bubbling streams,
Where every note, a memory seems.
In stillness wrapped, their echoes play,
In whispered hopes that gently sway.

As day unfolds, the laughter fades,
Yet in the heart, their presence wades.
A secret kept where stillness reigns,
In quiet corners, magic gains.

So, listen close, with open mind,
For sprite echoes are not hard to find.
In nature's arms, their spirits twirl,
A dance eternal in a timeless whirl.

The Lure of the Forest Floor

Amongst the roots where creatures dwell,
The forest floor holds stories to tell.
With every leaf that whispers low,
A tapestry of life does grow.

The mushrooms bloom in spots of light,
Their colors bold, a wondrous sight.
While creeping vines in shadows play,
An artful dance of green and gray.

Beneath the canopy, life's embrace,
A hidden world, a secret space.
Where sounds of nature softly hum,
And ancient wisdoms gently come.

Each pebble, moss, and ripple sings,
Of timeless paths and hidden wings.
The lure of earth, so rich and warm,
In every breath, the spirits swarm.

To wander here is to belong,
In nature's heart, one finds the song.
To tread upon this sacred ground,
Is to glimpse wonders yet unfound.

Tapestry of Moonlit Thickets

In thickets where moonlight softly gleams,
The shadows dance, entwined in dreams.
Whispers of night, a magic lore,
Guide the wanderers to the forest's core.

Branches weave tales, age-old and wise,
Under the gaze of starry skies.
The nightingale sings of a time long past,
Echoing secrets that forever last.

Moss blankets ground in emerald hues,
Murmurs of leaves, as soft as dews.
Silver beams paint the twilight fair,
And spirits of night weave through the air.

A tapestry spun with silken threads,
Of ancient roots and dreams long spread.
Beneath the boughs where shadows play,
Life stirs in magic, come what may.

Veils of Light in the Woodland Realm

In the woodland realm where silence reigns,
Veils of light weave through the lanes.
Golden rays peek through the trees,
Cascading down like gentle seas.

Every leaf shimmers in the sun's embrace,
Worn by time, yet full of grace.
A dance of dappled light and shade,
Crafts a paradise, nature made.

Ferns unfurl in a soft refrain,
To the hum of life, a sweet refrain.
Beneath the boughs, from dusk till dawn,
Nature's symphony plays on and on.

Fairies flit in the golden glow,
Tales of wonder only they know.
To dwell within this hallowed space,
Is to find a heart's warm embrace.

Echoes of the Mystical Undergrowth

In the mystical undergrowth, secrets dwell,
Where shadows breathe and stories swell.
A tapestry of roots entwined,
In whispers of dreams, the lost will find.

The forest hums with a mystic lore,
Echoes of creatures who've walked before.
Traces of footsteps, both faint and bold,
Guide the wanderers through the fold.

Murmurs of spirits drift on the breeze,
Carrying tales of ancient trees.
Softly they beckon, these hidden paths,
Awakening old echoes, stirring hearts.

Flickers of light between shadows play,
Creating a dance at the end of day.
Each rustling leaf, a song of the night,
Leading the soul to the dawn's first light.

Dappled Dreams in Nature's Cradle

In nature's cradle, dreams take flight,
Dappled shadows turn day to night.
A gentle hush fills the air,
Where magic lingers everywhere.

Petals soft as a lover's sigh,
Bask beneath the open sky.
The brook babbles secrets, sweet and low,
As time winds softly, letting go.

In twilight's blush, the world transforms,
Wrapped in wonder, the heart warms.
Every breath a gift, a fleeting chance,
To join the forest in its dance.

A symphony of nature, rich and rare,
Awakens the spirits lingering there.
Dappled dreams arise and shine,
In the cradle of woods, so divine.

The Glow of Hidden Realms

In shadows deep, where whispers dwell,
A magic stirs, a secret spell.
The moonlight dances on ancient stone,
Awakening dreams that linger, unknown.

Through ivy veils and silken mists,
The silhouettes of fate persist.
A lantern's glow, a guiding light,
Illuminates paths in the depth of night.

With every step, the heartbeats quicken,
Among the whispers where hopes are thickened.
A fortune spun in the fabric of time,
A tapestry bright, a melody's rhyme.

In hidden realms where shadows swoon,
The echo of laughter, a soft, sweet tune.
Through labyrinths woven of fragile thread,
A journey awaits where few dare to tread.

So heed the call of the unknown gleam,
For within the dark lies a shimmering dream.
Embrace the allure of the enchanted night,
Where stars are born from the myths of light.

Threads Woven in the Twilight

When twilight spills its golden hue,
The world transforms, both old and new.
A tapestry crafted in gossamer lace,
Embracing the shadows with a tender grace.

The whispers of time weave stories untold,
Of heroes and dreams, both timid and bold.
In the stillness, hearts begin to sway,
As twilight beckons, the night steals the day.

With each fleeting moment, the colors entwine,
We dance with the echoes of fate's design.
Underneath the stars, we find our place,
In threads of wonder, our souls interlace.

As night drapes its cloak, we gather our dreams,
Floating on currents of moonlit beams.
The fabric of magic unfurls in the dark,
In the realm of the twinkling, a spirited spark.

So treasure the twilight, both mystic and bold,
For there we discover the stories of old.
In every thin thread, an adventure awaits,
Where whispers of destiny weave through the gates.

Beneath the Arching Boughs

Beneath the boughs where the secrets sigh,
The heart of the forest breathes soft and shy.
Each leaf a tale, each branch a dream,
In the cool, shaded glow, imagination streams.

The roots hold the stories of ancients long gone,
In the tapestry woven, a bittersweet song.
An odyssey whispered in rustling leaves,
Where the spirit of magic gently weaves.

A murmured promise in the cool, crisp air,
Of wonder awaiting, treasures laid bare.
With every step taken on mossy trails,
The forest's embrace tells mystical tales.

Bathed in the light that trickles like rain,
We find our solace amidst joy and pain.
In the shadows where sunlight dares to intrude,
A sanctuary blooms where hearts can be renewed.

So linger awhile 'neath the arching trees,
Let the forest's charm wrap you like a breeze.
For in this haven, where whispers abide,
The essence of time flows like a gentle tide.

The Pulse of the Enchanted Soil

In the earth's embrace, a heartbeat resides,
Where magic dwells and solace abides.
The whispers of roots intertwine like a song,
In the pulse of the soil, we all belong.

Each grain tells a tale of day and of night,
Of journeys embarked on in search of the light.
The flowers of hope bloom in vibrant arrays,
In the cradle of nature, our spirits will blaze.

Beneath the surface, the mysteries swirl,
A dance of the elements, a wondrous whirl.
Each creature and leaf plays its part in the symphony,
A testament carved in the language of harmony.

The soil, a canvas of stories unspun,
Where the trials of time converge into one.
Together we rise, as petals unfold,
Embracing the warmth of the magic it holds.

So listen closely to the pulse deep below,
For in every heartbeat, the world starts to glow.
With nature's caress, we grow and we thrive,
In the enchanted soil, our dreams come alive.

Nature's Lattice and Lore

In the meadow where shadows play,
Each flower speaks, with whispers gay.
The sun weaves gold through branches high,
And dreams take flight, like birds that fly.

Ancient tales in the wind's soft sigh,
Of wandering souls and the night sky.
Leaves rustle secrets that morning brings,
Nature's magic in all small things.

Roots entwined in a dance of fate,
The forest holds her secrets straight.
Each rustling leaf a chapter told,
In stories written, in threads of gold.

Rivers sing with a gentle tune,
Reflecting stars, the sun and moon.
Mountains cradle the earth so wide,
In nature's arms, we can abide.

A weave of life, both bright and dim,
In every shadow, the light grows slim.
Yet in the dark, a spark remains,
Lattice of lore, where love sustains.

Dappled Dreams Under the Green

Beneath the boughs, in green's embrace,
Dappled light finds a secret place.
Where laughter dances on the breeze,
And whispers gather among the trees.

In twilight's fold, dreams gently gleam,
As starlit shadows weave through a stream.
Soft petals fall like wishes cast,
In the quilt of night, so slow and vast.

A carpet of moss, so rich and deep,
Where old tales flourish, and memories sleep.
Each step unveils a new delight,
In this realm where day surrenders night.

The golden sun, a friend unmasked,
Sings through leaves; a gentle task.
With every breath, the world feels keen,
A tapestry stitched, of vibrant green.

As shadows lengthen, the magic swells,
In every corner, adventure dwells.
So take a breath, weave in the light,
In dreams dappled, through the night.

Enigmas of the Whispering Woods

In the depths where silence reigns,
The woods conspire with soft refrains.
Each rustling branch a timeworn clue,
Of spirits past that wander through.

Echoes dance on the cusp of dawn,
In shadows deep, secrets are drawn.
Moonlight glimmers on paths untread,
Where even the brave may fear to tread.

The air is thick with tales untold,
Of hidden realms and magic old.
Each tick of time a whispered dare,
To seek the wonders hiding there.

Twisting vines like thoughts long spun,
Guard the lore of what's begun.
With ivy's touch and stone's embrace,
The forest holds its timeless grace.

With every step, a riddle unfolds,
In Nature's arms, where magic holds.
Through every twist, the heart shall see,
Enigmas dwell, both wild and free.

Footfalls of the Elfin Dancers

In moonlit glades, where shadows twine,
The elfin dancers weave and shine.
With laughter light, they spin and sway,
In harmony with the stars' ballet.

Barefoot under the shimmering night,
They trace the dreams in silvery light.
Each footfall leaves a magic trace,
A story spun in the quiet space.

With twirling skirts and golden hair,
They summon winds; they stir the air.
Every frolic a fleeting song,
In a world where wonders belong.

The forest hums a vibrant tune,
To which the delves and fae commune.
With every leap, the heart beats fast,
In moments caught, too quick to last.

When dawn appears, they fade from view,
But echoes linger, soft and true.
Leaving behind the night's expanse,
The whispered joy of their last dance.

Shadows of Gossamer Grace

In twilight's wane, the shadows play,
Gossamer whispers dance away.
Soft moonlight weaves through branches thin,
A tapestry of secrets, night begins.

The stars are cloaked in silken mist,
Each silver thread, a gentle tryst.
They cradle dreams on whispered sighs,
In every glance, a thousand lies.

A flicker here, a spark of gold,
In shadows deep, the stories told.
A world unseen, where magic sings,
In every corner, wonder clings.

As dawn approaches, colors blend,
The fragile night begins to end.
Yet still we feel the shadows' grace,
In every heart, they leave a trace.

So let us wander, hand in hand,
Through realms where dreams and shadows stand.
For in those depths, our spirits twine,
In gossamer grace, the stars align.

Mossy Veins and Hidden Dreams

Beneath the bark of ancient trees,
Mossy veins weave stories with ease.
In every crevice, a secret sleeps,
A world of whispers, where silence keeps.

Among the roots, the dreams entwine,
Hidden places, where hearts align.
Soft petals hold the morning dew,
And every step feels fresh and new.

A glimmer sparkles in the shade,
Promising wonders that never fade.
The earth breathes deep, its pulse so fine,
Mossy veins where dreams entwine.

Through winding paths, our hopes will roam,
In nature's cradle, we'll find our home.
With every breath, the magic gleams,
In every moment, we chase our dreams.

So let the forest guide our way,
Through mossy trails, we'll forever stay.
In hidden realms, where beauty thrives,
Among the wild, our spirit strives.

Secrets Tucked in Forest Breaths

In every sigh, the forest breathes,
Secrets tucked in emerald leaves.
With every rustle, tales unfold,
Of creatures bold and spirits old.

Hushed whispers dance on gentle trees,
A symphony carried on the breeze.
Underneath the vast, deep sky,
The ancient woods invite a sigh.

Among the ferns, the shadows creep,
A hidden world where dreams can leap.
With every step, a magic found,
In every heartbeat, nature's sound.

The mossy floor, a soft embrace,
Cradles stories of every place.
In twilight's glow, the secrets blend,
In forest breaths, our hearts transcend.

So wander on, where shadows dwell,
And listen close to the forest's spell.
For in the quiet, wisdom waits,
In every breath, the heart creates.

Luminous Threads of Enchantment

Through twilight's veil, enchantments glow,
Luminous threads in a gentle flow.
Each flicker holds a story bright,
A dance of dreams in the soft moonlight.

In hidden glades, where fairies play,
Magic whispers, guiding the way.
With every tide of shimmering waves,
The night unveils what fortune saves.

A tapestry of silver sparks,
Weaving songs in the evening parks.
In shadows deep, the wonders gleam,
Awakening hearts from slumbered dream.

So let us chase the glowing trails,
Across the cosmos, past starry veils.
For in the light, our spirits soar,
Through luminous threads, we seek for more.

With each new dawn, the magic stays,
In the glow of hope, in all our ways.
Through every heartbeat, every glance,
In threads of light, we find our chance.

Gossamer Trails of Sprightly Shadows

In twilight's glow, the shadows dance,
With gossamer threads that weave romance.
They flit on whispers, soft and light,
Chasing the moon, embracing the night.

Beneath the boughs where secrets dwell,
Sprightly echoes cast their spell.
Through mists of magic, they twirl and play,
In the heart of dusk, they softly sway.

Each footstep prints the velvet ground,
In the symphony of silence, they're profound.
Like fleeting dreams, they vanish fast,
Leaving a trace of the moments past.

Amid the trees, their laughter gleams,
In woven woods where daylight dreams.
They guide the lost, the brave, the true,
On gossamer trails where wishes brew.

Beyond the stars, the shadows rise,
A tapestry spun of starlit skies.
In wonder's grip, they forge the night,
With every flicker, a world of light.

Beneath the Foliage's Embrace

Amidst the leaves, where soft winds sigh,
Beneath the boughs, the secrets lie.
A whispered tale of earth's delight,
In nature's arms, all feels right.

The dappled sun through branches plays,
Casting patterns in golden rays.
Each rustle holds a mystery near,
Inviting all to pause and hear.

Whispers rise from the roots so deep,
Holding promises that the ancients keep.
The fragrance of earth, rich and pure,
Beneath the foliage, hearts endure.

A symphony hums in the vibrant fray,
As creatures lounge in the soft bouquet.
Each fluttering leaf sings a song,
In the embrace where we all belong.

When dusk descends with a spectral grace,
The woods awaken, a sacred space.
Beneath the foliage, time stands still,
A cozy haven, a gentle thrill.

Luminous Veins in Sylvan Soil

In sylvan soil, where secrets lie,
Luminous veins weave passages nigh.
With golden roots grasping the earth,
They cradle dreams, they fuel rebirth.

Glowing softly in moonlit haze,
They guide the wanderers through the maze.
Each heartbeat pulses within the ground,
In nature's cradle, solace is found.

Through whispers of wind, tales are spun,
Of the battles fought, the victories won.
In radiant hues, the life does bloom,
As shadows disperse, dispelling gloom.

With every drop of rain that falls,
The earth rejoices, its spirit calls.
Luminous veins in the dark do gleam,
A testament to every dream.

From roots to leaves, the magic flows,
In the rhythm of life, the story grows.
In sylvan soil, where wonders swell,
Each whispered truth a potent spell.

Enigma of the Hidden Whispers

In the heart of woods, an enigma stirs,
Hidden whispers drift on feathered furs.
Each word a shadow, softly spun,
In the tapestry woven, we come undone.

The breeze carries secrets through the glade,
Soft as a promise, a shifting shade.
The leaves hold tales of ages past,
In rustling murmurs, they silently cast.

Beneath the stars, the cosmos sighs,
An echo of truth in the midnight skies.
The night enchants with its silver tone,
In the silence, we find the unknown.

As dawn awakens, the whispers fade,
Leaving behind a magic parade.
Yet in our hearts, they linger still,
An enigma cherished, a timeless thrill.

So roam the woods, and you may find,
The whispers of nature, both gentle and kind.
In the rustling leaves, in the softest breeze,
The enigma waits, hidden with ease.

Fluttering in Twilight's Weave

In the hush where shadows play,
The fireflies start their dance,
With a soft and golden sway,
In twilight's fleeting glance.

Leaves whisper secrets overhead,
As stars blink into the night,
While dreams begin to spread,
In the softening light.

A silver mist spreads like a song,
Through the thicket's gentle grace,
Where the weary find they belong,
In this dusky, hidden place.

In the heart of the forest's fold,
Magic lingers in each breath,
Stories of the brave and bold,
Echoing beyond sweet death.

So dance, dear heart, in twilight's weave,
Let your spirit rise and soar,
For the night holds what we believe,
In dreams forevermore.

Cloaked in Nature's Gentle Hand

The morning breaks, the dew drops cling,
To petals soft and bright,
In the hush of dawn they sing,
Nature's pure delight.

A brook runs wild, a ribbon's gleam,
Through evergreens so tall,
It carries with it every dream,
In its gentle call.

Beneath the boughs, a world of peace,
Where whispers of the trees,
Bring heartache's burden sweet release,
In the softest breeze.

Each creature plays a timeless role,
In the circle of the day,
Where every heart and every soul,
Finds their secret way.

So let us walk with hearts in hand,
In nature's warm embrace,
In the dreams where we can stand,
Cloaked in her gentle grace.

Whispers of the Gnarled Elders

In the woods where shadows dwell,
The gnarled elders stand tall,
Holding secrets they won't tell,
Heed the whispers of their call.

Roots entwined with tales untold,
Branches arch like ancient pride,
In their gaze, the ages fold,
Guarding all that's deep inside.

Mossy robes and rugged bark,
Bear the weight of countless years,
In their shadows, bright and dark,
Reside both laughter and tears.

Listen close, as breezes weave,
Through the forest's breathing heart,
In their calm, you shall believe,
That all nature plays its part.

So tread with care where wisdom lies,
In the hushed and sacred lands,
For the whispers of their sighs,
Shape the world as time expands.

Tapestry of Sylvan Sighs

In twilight's glow, the colors blend,
A tapestry does unfold,
With every sigh that nature sends,
A story waiting to be told.

The leaves begin their gentle dance,
As breezes cross the boughs,
Nature's heart begins to prance,
In a world alive with vows.

Among the ferns, the shadows gleam,
Where the creatures come to play,
In the silence, they chase a dream,
As night softly turns to day.

With every breath, a magic thread,
Weaves through heartbeats, bold and bright,
In the forest, where all are led,
To seek the wonders of the night.

So let us linger in this place,
Where sylvan sighs entwine our souls,
For in this realm of timeless grace,
The tapestry of life unfolds.

Chill of the Veiled Dawn

The mist creeps in to curl and twist,
A shiver weaves through all it kissed.
The sun will rise, though wrapped in grey,
As shadows dance and gently sway.

The world awakes with bated breath,
In silence lingering, hinting death.
A whisper soft, the trees appear,
In quiet shades, they hold their fear.

The brook runs cold beneath the boughs,
While creatures pause, attentive, bows.
Each heartbeat echoes the plea,
Of dawn's cool touch, a mystery.

Yet in the stillness lies a spark,
A promise of the light in dark.
For every chill must yield to warm,
As hope transforms the veiled alarm.

Secrets Stirring in the Underbrush

In tangled roots and whispered leaves,
Where sunlight barely interweaves,
The hidden tales begin to breathe,
Within the thicket, secrets sheathe.

Each rustle hints of life unseen,
Where shadows skirt the thistle green.
A world of whispers soft and sly,
Where dreams take flight, yet never fly.

The heart of night keeps watchful eyes,
As moonbeams drift and softly sighs.
The brush conceals a dance of night,
In hushed tones, they share delight.

The path unfolds where none have trod,
Each step a prayer, a silent nod.
For mysteries, like fireflies,
Illuminate beneath the skies.

Hushed Conversations with the Trees

Beneath the boughs, secrets unfold,
In whispers warm, both shy and bold.
The ancient oaks, with ageless grace,
Hold stories of a sacred place.

The leaves exchange their timeless lore,
As gentle breezes stir and pour.
With every rustle, they unite,
In quiet talks of day and night.

The trunks embrace the life around,
In silence deep, wisdom is found.
While roots entwine beneath the ground,
A bond of earth, forever bound.

Their voices rise like songbirds' cheer,
Inviting all who care to hear.
For in the stillness, truths emerge,
As hearts and trees begin to merge.

Elfin Echoes of the Deep Woods

In shaded glades where shadows play,
The echoes of the elves hold sway.
With laughter light as gossamer,
They frolic where the dreamers stir.

The twinkling lights weave through the ferns,
A dance that tempts the heart and yearns.
With every step, the magic sings,
Of whispered dreams and ancient things.

In moonlit pools, reflections gleam,
The world awash in silver stream.
With every glance, a gentle nudge,
The deep woods hum, a hidden grudge.

For in the still, the echoes start,
A song that weaves within the heart.
A call to all who dare to roam,
In elfin lands, we find our home.

Whispers of Enchanted Roots

In the heart where shadows sigh,
Ancient whispers weave and fly,
Beneath the trees, their secrets dwell,
In every leaf, a magic spell.

Sparkling dew on emerald blades,
Glimmers of light through leafy shades,
Softly calling, the night invites,
For those who seek, in dreams, true sights.

A rustling breath, a gentle tease,
The forest hums with hidden pleas,
Each footstep stirs the sleeping dreams,
The roots adorn with silver beams.

Beneath the gaze of stars so bright,
A dance of shadows spins the night,
In every corner, mysteries hide,
These ancient woods, a timeless guide.

Shadows Among the Ferns

Beneath the ferns, the shadows creep,
Where secrets of the forest sleep,
A gentle breeze, a whisper faint,
Echoes of dreams, both wild and quaint.

Through tangled roots and twilight's glow,
The wisdom of the ages flow,
With every pause, the world stands still,
To listen close, to heed the thrill.

In the hush, where time is lost,
A soft reveal of phantom frost,
The spirits dance, they twist and sway,
In hidden glades, they laugh and play.

With every turn, a thought anew,
The past embraces what is true,
Among the ferns, old stories breathe,
In silent tales, we weave and seethe.

Ethereal Threads of the Glade

Threads of starlight, woven tight,
In the glade, a tapestry bright,
Each shimmer holds a tale untold,
In whispers soft, the night unfolds.

Bramble and bloom, a fragrant dance,
In the silence, a fleeting chance,
To trace the lines of fate and fate,
Where dreams awake, both small and great.

The call of owls, a haunting song,
Guide the lost where they belong,
Through velvet darkness, shadows glide,
In every breath, the past abides.

Magic on the breeze so light,
In every heart, a flickering light,
Ethereal threads that gently twine,
In the glade's embrace, we intertwine.

Secrets in the Hollow Earth

In deepened caves where silence reigns,
The echoes hold what time contains,
Through ancient paths in darkly hush,
The secrets call in hidden rush.

Candles flicker, shadows sway,
In twisting tunnels, lost astray,
The heartbeats thrum, a pulse divine,
In hollow earth, where wonders shine.

With every footfall on the stone,
The tales of old begin to moan,
Beneath the ground, a life unseen,
In every crack, the world's between.

The treasure sought is wisdom's might,
In depths of dark, emerges light,
Secrets weave through womb of earth,
In silence, we discover birth.

Of Myths and Whispered Roots

In shadows deep where whispers breathe,
Legends linger, stories wreathed.
An ancient tree with gnarled bark,
Holds secrets whispered in the dark.

Moonlight dances on silver dew,
With every step, a tale anew.
Roots that twist like fabled vines,
Unravel truths in hidden signs.

The owls hoot soft, the crickets hum,
While echoes call, the night's a drum.
Through brambles thick, the paths unfold,
Where myths are woven, brave and bold.

Beneath the stars where dreams collide,
With every turn, we must abide.
In every nook, a story glows,
Of whispered roots, the heart it knows.

The Heartbeats of the Wild Ones

In forests thick, where wild hearts roam,
Nature sings, our shared, wild home.
The pulse of life in each swift breath,
A symphony of life and death.

With bristlecone and oak so old,
Whispers of the brave and bold.
Hushed voices rise with wings in air,
Tales of freedom woven with care.

The brooklet laughs, the branches sway,
Inviting us to join the play.
A unity in shadows cast,
The wild ones dance, their spirits vast.

In every rustle, every sigh,
The echoes of the ages cry.
Nature's heart, a constant song,
Reminds us where we all belong.

Swaying with the Golden Ferns

Golden ferns in delicate fray,
Sway gently in the light of day.
A dance of green, a work of art,
Bringing solace to the heart.

Beneath the sun, their shadows play,
Creating dreams that drift away.
In whispers soft, they call our names,
Their secrets wrapped in nature's games.

A rustle here, a flutter there,
With every breeze, the wild declares.
The ferns, they sway, the world spins round,
In golden hues, true magic found.

Embrace the sway, the touch of light,
For every fern, a tale in flight.
Through verdant realms, our spirits rise,
Swaying gently 'neath the endless skies.

Hidden Tales of the Woodland Way

In woodland depths where shadows play,
Lies a path, the woodland way.
With every step, the stories breathe,
A tapestry of fate we weave.

Moss-covered stones, the light cascades,
Whispering dreams in sunlit glades.
Each turn reveals a tale untold,
Of adventures waiting, brave and bold.

The spirits rise with twilight's fall,
In every echo, hear their call.
Through tangled roots and branches wide,
Nature's heart opens, a guide.

Embrace the paths where tales entwine,
In the woodland's depths, our souls align.
Hidden truths await our gaze,
In the soft hues of the woodland haze.

Nature's Hidden Heartstrings

In the forest deep and wide,
Where secrets in the shadows hide,
Each leaf a whisper, soft and clear,
Plays the song that only we hear.

Above, the stars in velvet night,
Twinkle softly, a gentle light,
Guiding us through the tangled trails,
Where magic weaves in silent tales.

The river hums a lullaby,
As fleeting clouds drift softly by,
And every breeze that brushes past,
Carries memories that hold us fast.

Flora dances in morning's grace,
With dew-kissed petals we embrace,
Nature's heartbeat resonates,
In every moment, love awaits.

Beneath the boughs where shadows play,
We find our dreams in soft decay,
Each step we take, a story spun,
In nature's heart, we are as one.

Enchanted Whispers of the Grove

In twilight's glow where breezes sigh,
The ancient trees begin to pry,
Their branches sway with secrets steep,
As nighttime wraps the world in sleep.

The moonlight spills on mossy ground,
Where whispers float without a sound,
A symphony of life unseen,
In wild seclusion, pure and green.

Each rustling leaf, a tale unfolds,
Of timeless journeys, brave and bold,
A labyrinth of paths to roam,
In the grove, we find our home.

With every flicker of the stars,
The night reveals its hidden scars,
Yet beauty thrives in shadows dim,
An enchanted dance, a sacred hymn.

Together we weave through time and space,
In this embrace, we find our place,
With every heartbeat, truth we seek,
In whispers soft, the woods can speak.

Shadows Play Among the Stones

Underneath the grey stone arch,
Where shadows linger, keen to march,
The echoes of the past collide,
With every footstep, they confide.

The winds carry tales from afar,
Of battles won, of lost regard,
In the quiet, histories bloom,
As twilight fades, we chase the gloom.

Moss-crested rocks, a gentle throne,
Where the weary pause, all alone,
And in this stillness, wisdom sings,
Of ancient truths that time still brings.

Through cracks and crevices they creep,
Whispers of those long gone to sleep,
Yet in their silence, voices rise,
Painting portraits in the skies.

In this realm where shadows cast,
We find ourselves, both free and fast,
Among the stones, our spirits soar,
In every heartbeat, we explore.

Fern Fronds and Forgotten Dreams

Amidst the ferns, where shadows play,
Lie dreams once held, now far away,
Each frond unfurls, a tale to tell,
Of hopes and wishes woven well.

The sunlight dapples through the trees,
Awakening long-lost memories,
In the stillness, hearts can mend,
Where nature's soft embrace extends.

Each breath of air, a fleeting chance,
To weave our thoughts in a timeless dance,
And as the world begins to spin,
We find the strength to start again.

With every rustle, whispers sigh,
Of love and loss that's passed us by,
Yet in the glades where ferns entwine,
The seeds of hope begin to shine.

So let us stroll through nature's dream,
Where every thought can gently gleam,
In fern fronds deep, our souls will flight,
And touch the dawn in softest light.

Veins of Wisdom in the Earth

Deep within the soil's embrace,
Ancient stories softly trace.
Roots entwined in silent thought,
Secrets whispered, wisdom sought.

A touch of earth beneath the skin,
Life's history begins within.
Fossils tell of times long past,
In the stillness, shadows cast.

Lifeblood flows in veins unseen,
In the dark, where dreams convene.
From the crust to sky above,
Nature speaks of truth and love.

Each pebble holds a tale to share,
In this world of wild affair.
The mountains sigh, the rivers hum,
To the beat of earth's soft drum.

Listen close and heed the call,
In the silence, hear it all.
For in the soil, the heart does dwell,
Veins of wisdom, truths to tell.

Thin Whispers of Celestial Lore

Stars above in velvet night,
Whisper tales in soft moonlight.
Comets streak like dreams on fire,
Through the cosmos, hearts aspire.

The milky way, a river bright,
Carries whispers of the light.
Galaxies in silent flight,
Hold the universe's might.

In the hush of evening's glow,
Ancient secrets start to flow.
In the silence, soft and clear,
Echoes of the stars draw near.

Celestial beings, watch and weave,
In the tapestry we believe.
Orbs of wisdom, swirling high,
Granting wishes from the sky.

So gaze upon the heavens wide,
Feel the magic, let it guide.
For in the stars, a song of yore,
Thin whispers call forevermore.

The Lurking Light in Foliage

In the forest deep and dark,
Lurks a light, a fleeting spark.
Beneath the leaves, a glow ignites,
Guiding hearts through whispered nights.

With every step, the shadows dance,
In the glen, the spirits prance.
Roots and vines twist in delight,
As the moon dispels the night.

Crickets sing a haunting tune,
Drawing closer to the moon.
In the thicket, wonders bloom,
Where the hidden glories loom.

Wander far, let courage reign,
Embrace the wild, release the pain.
In the rustling leaves, find your way,
As the lurking light holds sway.

So let your heart be free and bold,
In the stories yet untold.
For in the emerald overgrowth,
The light reveals our silent oath.

Mysteries Linger in the Understory

Beneath the canopy's lush green,
Mysteries wait, seldom seen.
With whispers soft, they call your name,
In the shadows, hidden flame.

Fungi spread their webs of gold,
Guarding secrets, brave and old.
Twisting roots and gentle sighs,
Nature's lore beneath the skies.

In the underbrush, legends weave,
Hushed by winds that softly grieve.
Each rustle tells a tale concealed,
In the dark, their fate revealed.

The woodland spirits, shy yet wise,
Share their truths through ancient ties.
In the twilight, stories flow,
Of the life that beckons low.

So tread with care, for there you'll find,
Mysteries entwined, intertwined.
In the understory, life abounds,
In quiet magic, truth resounds.

The Veil of Verdant Mysteries

In emerald depths where shadows play,
Whispers of magic weave the day.
Ancient secrets softly sigh,
Wrapped in the leaves, the dreams float by.

Beneath the boughs of time-worn trees,
The gentle breeze stirs memories.
Each rustling leaf a tale untold,
Of daring hearts and treasures bold.

Mist hangs low in the twilight's glow,
Where fairy lights begin to show.
They flicker like stars in a midnight trance,
Luring the brave to join the dance.

A fawn with eyes of shining dew,
Guides the seekers, wise and true.
Through tangled roots, the path winds deep,
In the forest's hold, their secrets keep.

The veil of green, a magic screen,
Hides realms unseen, in shades serene.
With every step, the journey goes,
To realms where only the brave dare to chose.

Underneath the Elven Canopy

Beneath the leaves of silken sheen,
Elven whispers weave between.
Dappled light upon the ground,
Magic lingers all around.

A symphony of nature's tune,
Sings softly 'neath the silver moon.
Glimmers of hope in shadows cast,
Adventures call, both fierce and vast.

In glades where ancient shadows dance,
Time exists in a fleeting glance.
Each petal's sigh, each dewdrop's glow,
Tells of the paths where dreamers go.

Sprites a-flit on gossamer wings,
With laughter that forever rings.
Sparkling laughter, soft and light,
Guides the way through the velvet night.

The canopy holds a world apart,
Of longing, love, and brave new starts.
In every flicker, a tale held dear,
In the elven realm, all is clear.

Fibers of Forgotten Fables

Woven tales in twilight's thread,
Of heroes lost and dreams long fled.
Beneath the stars' watchful eyes,
Legends breathe, and time defies.

Old books lie in dust's embrace,
With yellowed pages, a sacred space.
Every word, a spell, a key,
Unlocking worlds where shadows flee.

A tapestry of whispers bare,
Threads of fate entwined with care.
Each stitch a story waiting to unfold,
Of brave hearts and secrets bold.

Echoes of laughter, warmth, and light,
In ancient gardens, spirits bright.
With every fiber, a story sewn,
Through ages past, it's gently grown.

The fables linger, a soft caress,
Each tale a whisper, a tender press.
In this realm of forgotten gleams,
Every heartbeat thrums with dreams.

Echoes in the Sylvan Silence

In the stillness, sounds of yore,
Whispers float on the woodland floor.
Echoes rise like soft-spun mist,
In the silence, truths persist.

Rustling leaves tell tales of night,
Of phantom forms and fleeting light.
Each breath of wind that drifts on by,
Carries secrets shared with the sky.

A brook's soft laugh, a distant call,
Beneath the boughs, enchantments fall.
In twilight's hush, the magic sways,
Binding hearts in twilight's gaze.

The wooden paths through shade and light,
Lead to dreams both bold and bright.
With gentle steps, the wanderers stray,
Through sylvan echoes, lost, they sway.

In every pause, a heartbeat found,
The silence swells, a sacred sound.
In the forest's heart, the silence reigns,
A world of wonder that still remains.

The Echo of Timeless Leaves

Amidst the whispering trees,
Shadows dance in the breeze.
Stories of ages untold,
In rustling leaves, they unfold.

Glimmers of gold in the sun,
Each flutter, a tale begun.
Nature's secrets, softly cast,
In echoes of leaves, the past.

Time tiptoes on gentle roots,
In silence, the forest Salutes.
Every branch a memory holds,
Each rustling whispers of old.

With every shift of the air,
The ancient spirits lay bare.
They linger where shadows meet,
In harmony, bittersweet.

Thus we wander, soul in hand,
Understanding their unspoken band.
In the echo of timeless sighs,
Nature's heart forever lies.

Unearthing Ancient Serenades

In the depths of the verdant glade,
Melodies of the past cascade.
Whispers swim through the air,
With every note, we lay bare.

Forgotten tunes, a soft refrain,
Each chord, a memory's gain.
Beneath the roots, stories weave,
In the harmony, we believe.

The crickets play a gentle tune,
Underneath the silver moon.
With each pluck and each strum,
The ancient rhythms hum.

Pausing to listen, hearts align,
In nature's song, we find rhymes divine.
Unearthing truths in the twilight's embrace,
Serenades lost not to erase.

Thus, we dance in this sacred space,
With reverence, we find our place.
In every note, the past ignites,
Weaving dreams through starry nights.

Nature's Composed Silvan Symphony

In every sigh of the swaying pines,
A symphony eternal aligns.
Softly strumming the heartstrings,
Nature sings of timeless things.

The brook bubbles a joyful hymn,
While sunlight dances on the brim.
Each element plays its part,
An orchestra of nature's art.

The rustle of leaves, a gentle drum,
With whispers of winds, our spirits hum.
The chirps and the croaks harmonize,
In this tranquil realm, wisdom lies.

Amongst the blossoms, a fragrant choir,
Fills the air with sweet desire.
Every petal, a note released,
Moments captured, hearts increased.

Thus, we listen, lest we forget,
The melodies that nature begets.
In this concert of life, we belong,
In nature's symphony, forever strong.

Under the Silent Canopy

Beneath the vast and woven shade,
A world where secrets never fade.
Among the branches, dreams reside,
In silence, the wistful abide.

Time pauses under the still embrace,
Each shadow holds a whispered grace.
Soft murmurs trail in the air,
Under the canopy, pure and rare.

With every step on the cushioned earth,
We find ourselves in the forest's mirth.
Hidden creatures speak in sighs,
Unveiling wonders beneath the skies.

The stillness cradles the hopes we keep,
In this tranquil shelter, nature's deep.
Each heartbeat synchronous with the trees,
Whispering tales on the gentle breeze.

So we wander, hearts open wide,
Under the canopy, there, we confide.
In the sacred silence, we genuinely see,
The magic that thrives, eternally free.

Roots of the Eldritch Grove

Beneath the shade where shadows cling,
Ancient whispers start to sing.
The roots entwine in secret waltz,
Guarding magic that never halts.

Sylvan spirits dance in light,
Beneath the moon, so pure and bright.
With every flicker, tales unfold,
Of battles lost and dreams of old.

The bark is thick, a riddle's prize,
Each knot conceals a world that lies.
In twilight's grasp, their secrets swell,
A story wrapped in nature's spell.

Brambles weave a tapestry,
Of lives entwined in harmony.
From roots to leaves, a song's embrace,
In every breath, a timeless grace.

As twilight hovers, shadows blend,
The secret paths that twist and bend.
In eldritch groves, where wonders play,
The heart of magic, night and day.

Sighs of the Sylvan Veil

Through curtain leaves, the breezes sigh,
With laughter light, they brush the sky.
Each rustling leaf a whispered tone,
A gentle dance, their secrets grown.

Moonlit paths weave soft and low,
Where spirits of the night would flow.
In shadows deep, their voices blend,
With every sigh, the night will send.

A veil of dreams, where dreams reside,
In sylvan realms, where hopes abide.
The echoes wrap around each tree,
In every heart, a melody.

With silver threads of starlit beams,
The world awakens from its dreams.
In tranquil woods, the sighs renew,
A symphony, both soft and true.

Beneath the boughs of emerald hue,
Sighs float like leaves that dance and strew.
Awake the heart to nature's call,
In sylvan veils, we'll find it all.

Hidden Harmonies of the Woodlands

In emerald depths where shadows play,
A harmony in whispers lay.
Each step on moss, a gentle tune,
Beneath the watchful eyes of moon.

The rustling reeds, they softly sway,
In secret dance, they find their way.
With every breath, the forest speaks,
In hidden groves, where magic peaks.

From acorn small to mighty oak,
The stories of the woodlands spoke.
In harmony, they all unite,
Creating symphonies each night.

A chorus built of earth and air,
Each note, a sigh, a whispered prayer.
In nature's choir, all voices blend,
A sacred bond that shall not end.

When dawn arrives with golden light,
These harmonies take graceful flight.
In hidden realms, the woods will sing,
Of magic, hope, and wondrous things.

Murmurs of the Hidden Realm

In twilight hush, the whispers swell,
From hidden realms, where shadows dwell.
A tapestry of ancient lore,
Each murmur beckons to explore.

When night descends, the fairies glide,
Through veils of mist, their secrets hide.
A world of wonders, shy yet bright,
Unveiling truths in the moonlight.

With every rustle, tales unfold,
Of hearts entwined and legends told.
Through winding paths and sparkling streams,
The hidden realm ignites our dreams.

In every sigh and soft refrain,
The echoes call through joy and pain.
A murmur weaves through leaf and root,
In nature's heart, the music's lute.

So wander deep where spirits roam,
In murmurs, find your truest home.
For in the whisper of the night,
The hidden realm reveals its light.

Life Under the Leafy Canopy

Beneath the boughs where whispers stir,
Life dances softly, a gentle blur.
Sunlight dapples on emerald hues,
Nature's secrets, old and new.

Branches cradle the evening song,
Where creatures gather, hearts belong.
A symphony of rustling leaves,
In this haven, the spirit weaves.

The breeze carries tales from afar,
Of starlit nights and the morning star.
Each root and petal in quiet grace,
Hold ancient stories in this space.

Camouflaged magic, vibrant and true,
In every corner, a vibrant view.
Life thrives in shadows, a sacred trust,
Under the canopy, a world of rust.

Glowing fireflies dance in delight,
As dusk unveils the cloak of night.
Here lies a realm, both wild and free,
Under the leafy canopy, we see.

Threads of Light Amongst Shadows

In murky depths, where shadows play,
Bright threads of light weave through the gray.
Dancing on edges of whispered dreams,
Life intertwines in silvery beams.

With hands of dusk and fingers of dawn,
The day unfolds as the night is drawn.
A tapestry woven with hope and fears,
The symphony sings of laughter and tears.

Amidst the darkness, a flicker remains,
Guiding lost souls through their whispered pains.
Together we wander, hand in hand,
Searching for solace in enchanted land.

The glow of truths shines bright and bold,
In tales of the brave and the tales untold.
Each heart a lantern, each soul a spark,
Lost threads of light brightening the dark.

In the embrace of night's soft sigh,
We find our purpose, we learn to fly.
Beneath the stars, we gently sway,
Threads of light weave a brand new day.

Frosted Flutes of Nature's Choir

In morning's grasp, the crystals gleam,
Nature awakens, alive with a dream.
Frosted flutes sing soft and clear,
The chorus of chill that draws us near.

Each branch adorned with icy lace,
A delicate touch, a quiet grace.
Whispers of winter in every sound,
In the heart of the woods, magic is found.

As sunlight kisses the frozen ground,
A symphony rises, a sweet, haunting sound.
Nature's breath, both sharp and bright,
Conducts a melody, pure delight.

With every note, the trees sway low,
To the rhythm of life in the frost and snow.
Birds flit and flutter, a joyous retort,
Frosted flutes echo nature's court.

In the stillness, a moment divine,
Where beauty lingers in every line.
Frosted flutes play in perfect time,
Nature's choir, a celestial rhyme.

Secrets in the Soft Earth

Beneath the soil, where shadows dwell,
Lie whispered secrets, a hidden spell.
Roots entwine in a silent prayer,
Bearing witness to every care.

In the softness, life begins anew,
Each seed a promise of morning dew.
Buried deep in darkness and clay,
Dreams unfold in their quiet way.

The heartbeat of nature lies within,
Where silent journeys of life begin.
In tangled webs and gentle grace,
The soft earth cradles time and space.

Echoes of laughter, lost to the years,
Fill the void with ancient cheers.
Here lies the past in layers of dust,
In secrets of earth, we place our trust.

With each new dawn, the cycle spins,
Life emerges, where silence thins.
Nature's whispers, a serenade,
In the soft earth, our dreams are laid.

The Web of Nature's Intrigue

In the heart of the glen, the whispers weave,
Threads of silver and green that never deceive.
Secrets nestled in oak, by the stream's gentle flow,
Nature's design, an enigma to show.

Beneath the wildflowers, shadows dance light,
Each petal a story, a flicker in flight.
The rustling leaves share their tales so complete,
Echoes of ancients in rhythms discreet.

Winding brambles entrap the moon's glow,
Tangled in dreams where the lost spirits go.
A tapestry bright, rich with colors untold,
Nature's own secrets, a marvel to behold.

The mist rolls in softly, a blanket of sighs,
Cloaking the world in ethereal ties.
A spark in the darkness, a flickering flame,
Each moment a treasure, each moment the same.

Unravel the threads of this intricate land,
Feel the pulse of the earth, the heartbeat so grand.
With every step taken, the mysteries bloom,
In the web of nature, find solace from gloom.

Tangles of the Otherworldly

In the twilight where shadows and starlight collide,
Whispers of magic in currents abide.
Caught in the tendrils of dreams yet to weave,
A realm filled with wonder, beckoning to believe.

Echoes of laughter on the edges of sight,
Strange creatures capering, lost in the night.
They twirl 'round the moonbeams, wild and ablaze,
In tangles of twilight, they dance through the haze.

Glimmers of stardust pour down like the rain,
Each droplet a promise, a joyful refrain.
With eyes that enchant, they lead with a smile,
Through corridors woven with shadows and guile.

Fingers of fog weave embraces so tight,
In realms of the otherworldly, hidden from sight.
A call of the ancients, a tune bittersweet,
Unraveling tales where the strange ones entreat.

Through thorns and through brambles, paths twist and arc,

Seeking the magic that's bright in the dark.
A journey of wonder, where fate intertwines,
In the depths of the night, where the otherworld shines.

Sylphs in Twilight's Embrace

Dancing on air, with laughter so clear,
Sylphs weave through the twilight, their presence sincere.

Each flicker of light, a giggle, a sigh,
As stars twinkle gently in the deepening sky.

Wings of gossamer brush past the trees,
A symphony rising on the whispering breeze.
These spirits of night, so playful, so free,
Invite every shadow to join in with glee.

They twine through the branches, in circles they spin,
Spinning the magic that dwells deep within.
In twilight's embrace, the world's softly huddled,
Each moment, a heartbeat, each breath gently cuddled.

With starlight as lanterns, they pierce through the dark,
Carving out pathways where dreams leave their mark.
Echoes of wonder within every glance,
The sylphs weave a spell, leading all to their dance.

When dawn breaks the spell, with its golden embrace,
The sylphs scatter softly, leaving not a trace.
Yet whispers of twilight linger still in the air,
A promise of magic that's ever so rare.

Beneath the Canopy of Whispers

Beneath the leaves where the breezes confide,
Whispers of nature in harmony glide.
In the silence, a heartbeat, a tremor of fate,
Awakening spirits in shadows sedate.

Moss carpets the ground, soft as a sigh,
Ferns unfurl gently, reaching for sky.
In this twilight haven, secrets entwine,
Nestled in roots where the fairy lights shine.

A glance through the branches reveals dreams unspun,
Fragments of stories, each the same, yet one.
Echoes of laughter, an age-long refrain,
In whispers of winds, there's joy and there's pain.

The canopies rustle with tales to be told,
Of wanderers lost and of treasures of old.
Where moonlight drapes silver across ancient barks,
And time flows like water, with ripples and arcs.

So pause for a moment, allow your heart's beat,
In the dance of the leaves, let your burdens retreat.
For beneath the canopy where wonders reside,
Lies the essence of magic, where dreams coincide.

The Ballet of Subterranean Spirits

In twilight's hush, they twirl and glide,
With whispers soft, the shadows bide.
Their twinkling eyes like stars align,
In caverns deep, where secrets shine.

Their laughter echoes, light as air,
Each pirouette a fleeting flare.
They weave a tale of night and stone,
In silent worlds, where dreams are sown.

Among the roots, their dance unfolds,
With ancient grace, the past beholds.
They paint the darkness, bright and bold,
As time stands still, their story told.

Ethereal forms in moonlit beams,
They twine with fate, through woven dreams.
With every step, the earth they soothe,
In gentle rhythm, they find their groove.

So when you tread on hallowed ground,
And hear their tunes, a haunting sound,
Know that beneath, the spirits play,
In ballet's grace, they find their way.

Threads of Magic in the Moss

Beneath the trees, where shadows weave,
A tapestry of dreams to believe.
In emerald depths, the magic sighs,
As tiny wonders dance and rise.

The mossy beds, like velvet clime,
Hold whispers of the ancient rhyme.
Threads of light in every seam,
A fabric stitched with nature's dream.

With gentle hands, the fairies spin,
Their silken paths, the stories begin.
Each strand a wish, a heartfelt plea,
Entwined forever in harmony.

The trickle of a stream nearby,
Carries secrets that never die.
In silvery notes, the magic flows,
In twilight's breath, the wonder grows.

So wander softly, tread with care,
In mossy realms where hearts lay bare.
For every thread of nature's art,
Weaves a spell and binds the heart.

Subtle Hues of Forgotten Realms

In twilight's embrace, colors gleam,
Shadows dance, and the echoes dream.
A palette rich with layers deep,
Secrets hidden, in silence, keep.

The forests breathe in hues of yore,
While timeless tales tread evermore.
With gentle strokes of nature's brush,
They paint the past in a vibrant hush.

Each leaf a canvas, stories told,
In whispers soft, the brave and bold.
Among the ferns, the colors blend,
In quiet corners, where dreams transcend.

The twilight sky, a canvas rare,
A fleeting glimpse of magic there.
The shifting shades, a dance of fate,
Invite the heart to contemplate.

So linger long where echoes play,
In gentle hues that guide the way.
For in the stillness, truth reveals,
The subtle beauty that time heals.

The Dance of Life Under the Canopy

Beneath the boughs where sunlight spills,
Life thrums alive, with distant thrills.
In every rustle, a tale begins,
As nature's choir softly sings.

The branches sway, a rhythmic beat,
While creatures join in the grand retreat.
Frogs serenade in twilight's glow,
As shadows mingle with the flow.

The petals flutter, colors bright,
In harmony with the fading light.
A waltz of life, both fierce and kind,
Each moment stitched, interlined.

The whispers weave a gentle air,
Through spiraled paths, where spirits care.
In every fold, within each leaf,
Resides a truth beyond belief.

So step beneath the verdant dome,
And find in dance, a place called home.
For life unfolds in every sway,
In nature's arms, we find our way.

Laced with Moonlit Memories

In the hush of night, soft whispers weave,
Dreams take flight as shadows conceive.
Stars gleam bright, like lumined lace,
Each twinkle holds a long-lost place.

Winds recount tales of forgotten years,
Bathed in silver, washed of tears.
The moon hangs low, a guiding pearl,
In its glow, old stories unfurl.

Rustling leaves share secrets sweet,
With every step, the heart skips a beat.
Paths illuminated by a ghostly light,
Leading the way through the velvet night.

Time flows gently, like a flowing stream,
Moments captured in a starlit dream.
Memories dance where shadows dwell,
In the realm of magic, all is well.

As dawn approaches, the whispers fade,
Yet in our hearts, their traces stayed.
Laced with moonlit memories dear,
We carry with us what we hold near.

Roots in the Realm of Faery

Deep beneath the woodland's shade,
Life unfolds in secret glade.
Roots entwined like lovers' hands,
Whispering dreams of ancient lands.

In twilight's breath, magic breathes free,
Hidden realms call out to thee.
Starlit petals paint the ground,
In the stillness, enchantment's found.

Elusive sprites in dances twirl,
Through the underbrush, listen and whirl.
The aroma of earth, a fragrant sigh,
Where the faery folk with laughter fly.

Gleaming stones hold stories untold,
Mysteries wrapped in hues of gold.
Each heartbeat echoes in the trees,
As nature hums a timeless breeze.

A glimmering path leads far away,
Through fields where wildflowers sway.
Here in the wild, souls softly meet,
Roots in the realm of faery's heartbeat.

Secrets of the Emerald Earth

Beneath the soil, life thrives unseen,
Whispers of ancient, emerald green.
Secrets held in every stone,
In the cradle of nature, we're never alone.

Ferns unfurl like tales of old,
In shadows cast, their stories unfold.
Mossy carpets cushion our tread,
Nature's whispers, softly said.

Glistening streams song, they sing,
Of hidden treasures the earth will bring.
In every root, a wish resides,
Carried forth with the turning tides.

The heartbeat thrums in the ground below,
Where dreams are planted and seeds will grow.
Each rustle, a promise, each shiver, a spark,
Tales entwined with the dusk and the dark.

The emerald cloak of life entwines,
In hushed corners where magic twines.
Secrets of the earth persist,
In every glance, let wonder exist.

Murmurs from the Leafy Abyss

In the heart of the forest, where shadows play,
Murmurs drift softly, leading astray.
Leaves whisper secrets in a tender breeze,
Filling the air with stories that tease.

Beneath the branches, echoes of lore,
Tell of the whispers from ages before.
Ancient oaks stand guard with pride,
Holding the tales that time cannot hide.

Where sunlight dapples on emerald hue,
Glades beckon softly, inviting the new.
In the hush, a heartbeat thrums,
As nature calls, the wandering comes.

Each rustle speaks of life's embrace,
Murmurs of magic, beauty, and grace.
With open ears, let your spirit roam,
In the leafy abyss, find your home.

For in each leaf, a world awaits,
Messages written in fates and craters.
Murmurs from the depths of green,
Invite you to dance in the spaces unseen.

Dreaming in the Mossy Glade

Beneath the towering trees so high,
In the mossy glade where secrets lie,
Whispers of magic weave through the air,
As dreams take flight without a care.

Softly the ferns in twilight sway,
Holding the echoes of light's ballet,
While silvered beams touch the forest floor,
Inviting hearts to discover more.

Gentle streams with laughter flow,
Carving paths only fairies know,
Their glimmering dance, a sight so rare,
Enchanting souls, unraveling despair.

Within the thickets, shadows play,
Guardians of night, they weave and sway,
As twilight deepens, mysteries unfold,
In whispers of silver and threads of gold.

So linger awhile in nature's embrace,
Amidst the whispers, find your place,
And dream of wonders, both vast and grand,
In the mossy glade, where spirits stand.

Threads of Ethereal Essence

In the hush of night, the world entwines,
With threads of magic, the heart defines,
Ethereal whispers float through the dusk,
Binding the silent with glittering husk.

Glimmers of starlight, soft as a sigh,
Dance on the edges where shadows lie,
Each flicker a promise, each spark a tale,
Woven in silence, where dreams prevail.

Mysterious forces in gentle embrace,
Guide us through time, through space, through grace,
With every heartbeat, the magic flows,
Threads of essence that no one knows.

Look to the moon, that silvered face,
Illuminating paths to a hidden place,
For in the night, the spirit roams,
Creating a tapestry of whispered homes.

So follow the thread, let your heart lead,
In the realm of dreams, plant the seed,
And watch it blossom through shadow and light,
In ethereal echoes of the night.

The Dance of Sylvan Shadows

Beneath the arching boughs so wide,
Sylvan shadows in grace abide,
They twirl and spin on carpet of green,
In a dance of secrets, subtle and keen.

The moonlight gleams on silvery leaves,
As the forest sighs and softly breathes,
In this magic hour, enchantments swell,
Wrap the heart in their silent spell.

Branches entwined, a delicate lace,
Fingers of light in a warm embrace,
Each movement a story, a soft refrain,
Echoing laughter through the quiet lane.

Crickets drum a rhythmic tune,
As night descends like a velvet boon,
Guiding the shadows to dance and play,
In the forest's heart, where spirits stay.

So heed the call of the sylvan night,
Join the shadows in their flight,
For in their dance, the world aligns,
In whispered dreams where magic shines.

Hidden Paths in Twilight Hues

Along the trails where twilight weaves,
Lie hidden paths beneath the leaves,
Crimson and gold in the fading light,
Calling adventurers into the night.

In every turn, a story waits,
Of ancient woods and whispered fates,
Footsteps echo, soft and slow,
Guided by stars that start to glow.

With rustling leaves, the old ones speak,
Of fleeting moments, tender and weak,
They beckon the brave, the kind, the true,
To wander these paths of twilight hues.

Lanterns of fireflies guide the way,
Through meadows where night flowers sway,
An adventure awaits at every breeze,
As secrets unravel with effortless ease.

So take a chance, let wonder soar,
Embrace the magic that lies in store,
For on these hidden paths, half-known,
Your heart may find a place called home.

www.ingramcontent.com/pod-product-compliance
Ingram Content Group UK Ltd.
Pitfield, Milton Keynes, MK11 3LW, UK
UKHW021403230125
4267UKWH00036B/343